THE WORLD BENEATH OUR FEET

The Story of Soil

MESSNER BOOKS BY MARTIN L. KEEN

THE WORLD BENEATH OUR FEET
The Story of Soil
HUNTING FOSSILS
LIGHTNING AND THUNDER

Keen
The world beneath our feet

R
J
631.4
nc
2

DATE DUE

SE 9				
OC 15				

Northwest Wisconsin Library System

Vaughn Public Library

502 West Second Street
Ashland, Wisconsin 54806

Phone 682-3883

DEMCO

THE WORLD BENEATH OUR FEET
The Story of Soil

by MARTIN L. KEEN

Illustrated by
Haris Petie
and with photographs

JULIAN MESSNER   NEW YORK

Published by Julian Messner, a Division of Simon & Schuster, Inc.
1 West 39 Street, New York, N.Y. 10018. All rights reserved.

Printed in the United States of America

Copyright © 1974 by Martin L. Keen

Photos courtesy USDA
Soil Conservation Service, and the author

Design by Marjorie Zaum

Library of Congress Cataloging in Publication Data

Keen, Martin L.
   The world beneath our feet: The story of soil.

   SUMMARY: An introduction to soil, its formation, importance, conservation, various kinds, and the plant and animal life found in it.
   1. Soil science — Juvenile literature. [1. Soils] I. Petie, Haris, illus. II. Title.
S591.3.K43   631.4   74-7148
ISBN 0-671-32673-2
ISBN 0-671-32674-0 (lib. bdg.)

To
that
sturdy one with the questioning eyes,
daring all-fours stairs climber,
talker of a one-word language with a thousand inflections
Ross,
beloved grandson

CONTENTS

CHAPTER

1	What is Soil?	9
2	The First Soil	11
3	New Soil in the Making	21
4	Soil Horizons and Kinds of Soil	28
5	The Living Soil — I: Animals	35
6	The Living Soil — II: Plants	43
7	The War for Soil	52
8	Soil Science	63
9	Raindrops are Bombs	72
10	The Modern Use of Soil	84
	Glossary	90
	Index	94

Earthworms, insects, centipedes, grubs, dead leaves, pebbles, and vast numbers of living things too small to see—all in a great tangle—make a spadeful of soil a small world at your feet.

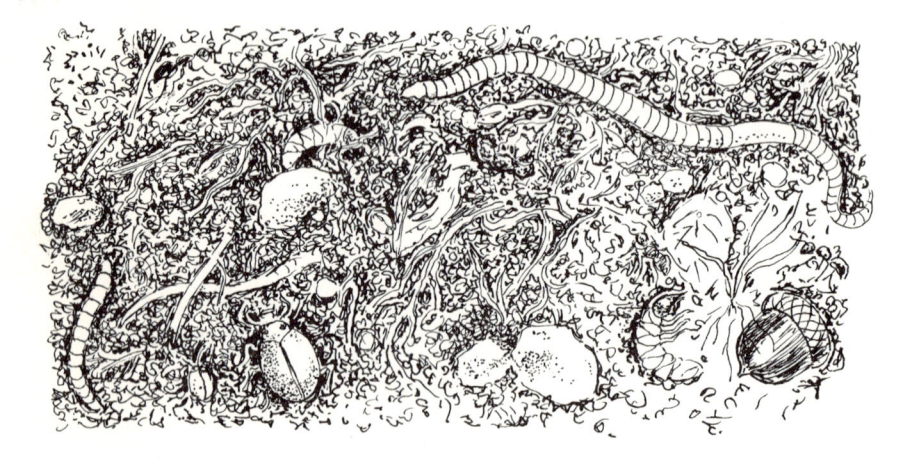

1
WHAT IS SOIL?

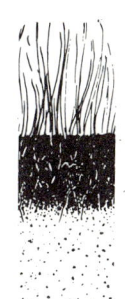

Dig up a spadeful of grassy soil. Turn it upside down and look at it closely. What a jumbled mass of small particles and tangled strands! And see the small living things moving within the jumble. There are millions of living and nonliving things in the little mound of soil. It is a kind of small world.

But what is soil? It is different things to different people. To an engineer, soil is the part of the earth's surface that is not water or solid rock. Soil is something on which to build a bridge, a roadway, or a house. Or soil is just something he must remove before putting the foundation of a building on the rock beneath.

To a farmer, soil is the top five or six inches of the ground in which he plants his crops. A wise farmer knows what kinds of soils make up his fields, so he can plant crops that grow best in each kind of soil. And he knows how he can keep his soil producing good crops.

To a soil scientist, soil is a complicated mixture of nonliving things, such as sand grains and smaller rock particles; decaying materials that come from dead plants and animals; and living things, both plants and animals.

The soil scientist shares the farmer's interest in seeing good crops grow in good soil, and knowing what makes some soils better for growing crops. He wants to know how many different kinds of soil there are, where they come from, and where they are found. He also studies the great number of different things that live in the soil. In this book, we will look at soil as if we are soil scientists.

2
THE FIRST SOIL

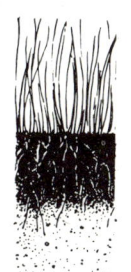

The Earth's Crust

The earth did not always have soil. It took many processes, working throughout hundreds of millions of years, to make the first soil.

Most scientists agree that there was a time when the earth was a ball of extremely hot, molten rock. The melting of the earth and then the cooling of its outermost region took at least a thousand million years. At the end of this immense span of time, the earth had cooled enough to form a crust of solid rock several miles thick.

Then the first process in the making of soil began: the rocky surface of the earth began to break up. It was pierced by volcanoes that spewed lava down their sides and flung large amounts of ashes into the air. Changes in temperature caused rocks to split. Earthquakes shook mountains, and pieces of rock tumbled and slid down mountainsides. The falling, sliding rocks shattered into pieces of all sizes.

These events, continuing for hundreds of millions of years, covered the lowlands and filled the valleys with rocks. These ranged in size from sand grains and very small dust particles to larger pieces, up to boulders. Winds blew the dust particles and sand grains back and forth across the earth's hot, dry rock-strewn crust.

Volcanoes like these were among the first forces to break the rocky surface of the young earth and begin the soil-making process.

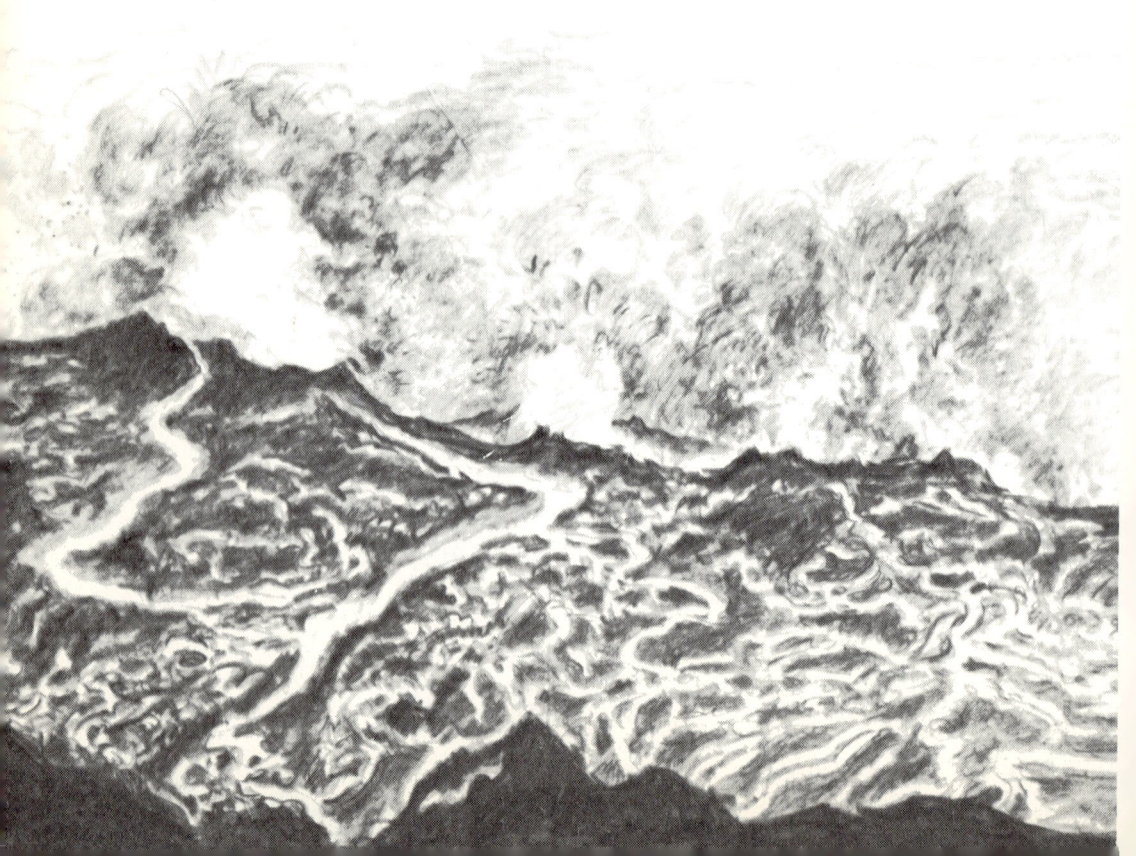

The Ocean and the Continent

The dust and sand storms that took place on the earth's still very hot surface were hidden in darkness. Occasionally, there was light from volcanoes and frequent flashes of lightning. Overhead, a vast cover of clouds miles thick prevented the sun's rays from penetrating to the rocky surface of the earth. Violent thunderstorms bombarded the earth with lightning bolts, and the rumble of thunder never ended. Torrents of rain fell, but the earth remained dry. Most raindrops evaporated in the air, which was heated by the very hot earth. Any raindrops that might have reached the earth's surface boiled upward in steam, rejoining the clouds from which they came.

Eventually, the cooling crust reached a temperature low enough to allow rain to remain on the bare rock. Rainwater, forming streams and rivers, ran to low-lying regions. The water gathered in large pools that increased in size, joined, and finally made up an immense ocean. This ocean covered nearly three-quarters of the earth's surface. A vast highland remained above the water. This land made up a single huge continent as big as all of the present-day continents put together. (Later, this great continent split apart, and the pieces began to move slowly across the earth's surface. These large pieces are the continents of today.)

As more and more rainwater remained on earth, the clouds became thinner and thinner. Finally, the cloud cover broke up. Areas of clouds formed here and there, and were blown through the atmosphere by winds, just as they are today. With sunlight reaching the earth's surface during each turn of the earth on its axis, there was night and day. The sun always shone on some part of the earth. Each year, as the earth revolved around the sun, the amount of sunlight changed regularly;

the earth now had seasons. There were warm and cool seasons, wet and dry seasons. In each season, there were warm days and cool nights, rainy days and dry, sunny days. The happenings we call weather had begun.

Weather, with its changes in temperature and wetness, became another cause for the breaking up of the earth's rocky crust. The running of rivers and streams across continents introduced erosion, another natural force that breaks up rock into small pieces. Eventually, the great amount of very small bits of rock, which covered the huge continent, provided one of the two ingredients needed for forming soil.

The First Soil

Although no one knows exactly how life began, scientists agree that it began in the ocean, about 2,500 million years ago. Two thousand million years later, the ocean was teeming with thousands of different kinds of plants and animals. All lived in water — either in the ocean or in rivers and streams.

About 500 million years ago, plants covered much of the land. Where there are land plants, there must be soil. But how did the rock dust in the lowlands and valleys become soil? Scientists still do not know exactly how, but some of them do have theories.

One theory points out that today soil is being formed in places where the earth's surface is bare rock. Therefore, the first soil may have been formed in the same way.

Lichens

It is very common to find plants called *lichens* growing on bare dry rock. But how does a lichen live without soil or water? The answer is that a

Lichen living on bare rock.

Second type of lichen living in soil formed by first lichen.

Moss living in soil made by lichens.

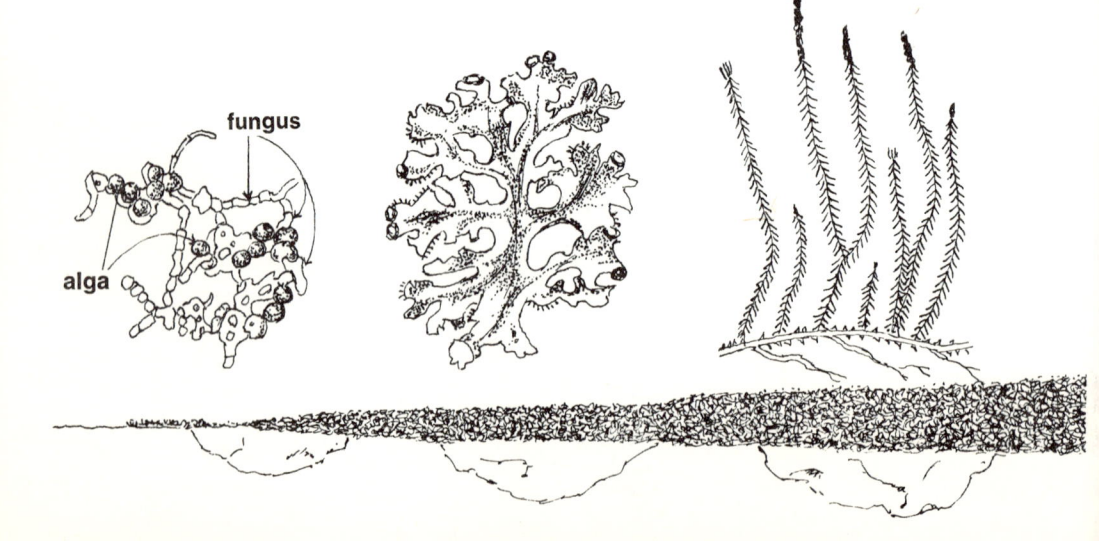

fungus

alga

lichen actually is made up of two plants: an *alga* and a *fungus.*

An alga is a plant that belongs to the group of plants called *algae.* The green scum you see sometimes on the surface of a pond and the slimy green covering on the shady sides of trees are algae. Or you may have seen algae in the form of the green or brown slippery mass of hairlike strands on rocks washed by the ocean. Algae contain *chlorophyll.* This is a substance that enables a plant to make its own food by using water and carbon dioxide from air, and energy from sun-

Grass living in soil made by lichens and moss.

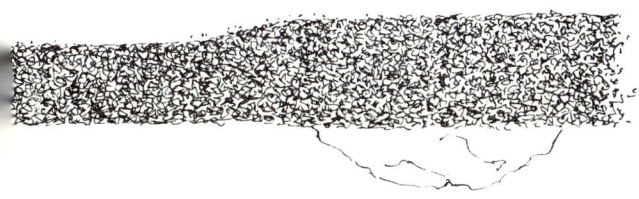

light. Algae cannot live very long without water.

A fungus is a plant that belongs to the group called *fungi.* Mushrooms and bread mold are two kinds you probably know. Fungi do not contain chlorophyll, and therefore cannot make their own food. They get their nourishment from live or dead plant and animal materials upon which they grow. Some fungi can live with extremely little water. They can take moisture from damp air or use tiny bits of water from the damp surface of a rock.

The alga and the fungus that make up a lichen take care of each other's needs. The fungus supplies the alga with moisture. The fungus takes nourishment from the alga, devouring some of it, but not enough to starve it or even hurt the alga very badly.

Although both algae and fungi lived in the ocean, scientists do not know whether they began their partnership as lichens in the ocean or whether it began on land. Let us guess that there were no lichens in the ocean.

An Important Accident

Perhaps, then, at the time when there were not yet any land plants, some kinds of algae grew on rocks washed by ocean tides, just as some seaweed algae do today. Now suppose that during one high-tide season, the *spores* of some kind of fungus were carried by waves onto algae-covered rocks. (A spore is a living cell that acts like a seed; if it is in favorable conditions of moisture and temperature, it will begin to grow into a new plant.) The season's high tides slowly receded, leaving fungi spores entangled in the algae on dry rocks. The algae began to dry up and die. Meanwhile, the fungi spores grew into fungus plants, using some of the algae for food. The fungi, taking moisture from the air or from fog-dampened rock, supplied water to the remaining algae, keeping them alive. In this way, the partnership we call a lichen might have begun.

Lichens, not needing the water of the ocean, were able to spread over bare rock, far inland. There, rock dust that ordinarily would have blown away became caught in the rough, moist surface of a lichen. When lichens died, the dead plants dried and eventually broke up into dust. But this was a new kind of dust. Unlike rock dust, it was made up of once-living materials. It was the second ingredient needed to make soil. Lichen dust mixed with rock dust may have been what formed the earth's first soil.

Not long after, decay-causing bacteria were added to the soil-making process. We know that decay bacteria lived in the ocean. Perhaps a high tide washed some of these bacteria onto a lichen-covered rock. Now the dead lichens could be broken down by the process of decay. With the addition of bacteria, the soil-making process was complete.

As millions of years passed, new land plants came into being. When they died, they added their once-living material to the soil-making process. In about 50 million years — a short time in the earth's long history — this process had carpeted most of the land with soil.

3
NEW SOIL IN THE MAKING

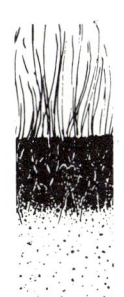

New soil is continuously being made today. Natural processes break rocks into tiny pieces which become rock grains and rock dust. Dead plants and animals decay and become small bits of once-living matter. The decayed material and the bits of rock become mixed together and form soil.

Weathering

The natural processes that break up rock are called *weathering*. This is the slow destruction of rocks by weather — day-to-day changes in temperature, rainfall, wind, and humidity. Weathering works slowly. It takes hundreds or thousands of years for a rock the size of a football to be broken into grains and dust.

If you want to see how weathering does its work, look at the gravestones in a cemetery. You

The tombstone on the left is older, but it has resisted weathering better.

will see how the sharp edges of the words on the older gravestones have been destroyed. On some of the gravestones that are more than 150 years old, you may not be able to read the words at all. There are two main kinds of weathering, and both eventually destroy rocks — or gravestones cut from rock.

Mechanical Weathering

Mechanical weathering changes the size and shape of rocks by breaking them into small pieces. Here is how it works.

22

Suppose rainwater collects in a crack in a rock. Then the water freezes. Water expands (increases in volume) when it changes to ice. This may cause the freezing water to push on the sides of the crack with enough force to split the rock. Usually, the crack is no wider than a thread, and the piece of rock that splits off is the size of a small bread crumb. This process goes on year after year, and a large rock can completely disappear, as it is broken into thousands of very small pieces.

Daily temperature change is another cause of mechanical weathering. Sun may heat the surface of a rock quite hot. As the heat slowly moves into the inner parts of the rock, the heated rock expands. When the sun sets, the surface of the rock cools quickly, but the inner parts do not. The rapidly cooling surface contracts (shrinks), while the inner parts remain warm and expanded. As a result, parts of the shrinking surface pull away from the rock beneath them and split off. This kind of weathering may happen anywhere, but it takes place most frequently in deserts and on high mountains, where the days are hot and the nights are cold.

One other way in which rocks break up into small pieces is simply by being knocked against each other. The soil beneath a rock on a hillside

Soil loosened by rain frees rocks, allowing them to roll down hill. These rocks may strike others, chipping off small pieces that eventually become part of soil.

may be washed away by rain. The rock rolls down the hill, striking other rocks on the way down. The striking together of the rocks chips pieces off them. These small pieces go into the soil-making process.

Chemical Weathering

Chemical weathering breaks up rocks into the materials of which they are composed (made up). Chemical weathering causes the rocks to *de*compose.

The very small amount of carbon dioxide gas in the air plays an important part in this process. The carbon dioxide dissolves in raindrops. The combination of carbon dioxide and water makes *carbonic acid.* Although carbonic acid is a weak acid, it can dissolve rock materials if it is given enough time. This means that, over a long time, rainwater can dissolve rocks.

The Destruction of Dead Things

Dead plants and animals are broken up into bits in several ways. The once-living material may become very dry and brittle like a dead leaf. It then crumbles because of its own weight, or it breaks apart if it is touched by any living things.

Dead plants and animals are also attacked by

Silhouettes of three dead leaves, showing how they are being cut into small pieces as mites, insects, bacteria, and fungi devour them.

many kinds of living creatures. Large animals, such as deer and cattle, chew leaves, twigs, and grass, dropping pieces on the ground. Smaller animals, such as mice, eat corn, wheat, and other seeds. They leave the seed coats in their burrows or on the ground.

Still smaller animals — the insects — bite, chew, and tear dead plants and animals. So do worms, centipedes, and mites.

Molds and other fungi grow upon the dead material, digesting some of it. The smallest of all plants — bacteria — grow on dead matter and complete its destruction. The fungi and bacteria secrete (give off) fluids that cause chemical changes to take place in the once-living matter. It is broken down into simpler chemical substances. Some of these are gases, which mix with air. Others dissolve in water and are absorbed by soil. All these actions are parts of the process called *decay*.

Decay may be fast or slow. In moist, hot climates, decay bacteria can destroy a small leaf in a few days. In dry climates, the same leaf might last for years. Usually, though, before dead matter is completely destroyed by decay, it is buried under new layers of dead plant and animal matter.

Although the main work of destroying dead things is done by living plants and animals, some of this work is done by nonliving processes. One of these is *oxidation*, which is the chemical combination of the oxygen in the air with any other substance. Oxidation may be fast, as in the burning of a log; or oxidation may be very slow, taking years to destroy a log as it lies on the floor of a forest. Dead materials that are being destroyed by oxidation are usually being destroyed at the same time by decay, which is faster.

All the soil-making processes are at work every second of every day. Each year, hundreds of millions of tons of new soil are made. Yet, at the end of each year, there is less soil than at the beginning. Human beings, as we shall see, destroy soil faster than nature can make it.

4
SOIL HORIZONS AND KINDS OF SOIL

In many places, roads have been cut through hills, leaving banks of earth exposed to view. If there is a place like this near where you live, take a careful look at the earth on the sides of the cut. Examine the top first. You will see that it is made up of pieces of leaves, blades of dead grass, bits of roots, and pieces of small twigs. There are also parts of insect bodies and many dead seeds. Look closely. You will see that many of these things are beginning to fall apart. They are rotting and decaying.

Now look a few inches below the top. If you can, dig out a piece of earth. You will see that you cannot recognize the leaves, grass, twigs, and insect parts any more. This is because they are so completely decayed. Rub some of this soil between your fingers and thumb. Feel the grit. It is made up of rock grains and rock dust. If you poke around, you should find some live insects and several kinds of worms.

Soil Horizons

Farmers and gardeners call the top layer of soil *topsoil*. It is the part of the soil in which they plant seeds. Soil scientists call topsoil the *A-horizon*. It is not possible to say how deep the A-horizon is. In some places there may not be any topsoil at all, because rain has washed it away or bulldozers have scraped it off. In other places, topsoil may be more than 15 feet deep.

This soil profile shows an A-horizon (topsoil) about one foot deep, a B-horizon also one foot deep, and a C-horizon at least two feet deep.

The next layer of soil is the *B-horizon.* It is made up of all one kind of material and is much firmer than the A-horizon. You may find tree and bush roots that have grown down into the B-horizon, but you will not find decaying organic matter.

Dig out some of the B-horizon, crumble it, and examine it. You will see bits of rock, grain-size and larger. These small pieces are made up of rock materials that resist weathering by rainwater that seeps down through the soil. Most of these bits of rock are quartz.

In places that have a damp climate, rainwater carries down into the B-horizon minerals that come from rocks weathering on the surface of the soil. Also, the water carries down dissolved materials from decaying organic matter.

In places where the climate is dry, water quickly evaporates from the surface of the soil before much of it can seep very far down. The evaporating water is replaced by water seeping upward from underground streams. The rising water carries dissolved minerals upward into the B-horizon. Because dissolved minerals move both upward and downward into the B-horizon, it is called the *zone of accumulation.*

If engineers had to blast through rock to make the road cut you are examining, you should be able to see the *C-horizon*. This layer will be at the top of the solid rock, or *bedrock*. The C-horizon consists of pieces of rock that have been either broken by blasting or split off the bedrock because of weathering. The blasted rocks have sharp edges. Those that have been weathered out of the bedrock have rounded edges and perhaps a pitted, rotten look.

Weathering of rock deep underground is different from weathering that takes place on the surface. Except in the very coldest parts of the earth, day-to-day — or even season-to-season — changes in temperature do not take place more than about a foot below the surface. So, bedrock is not weathered by freezing and by quick temperature changes. It is chemical weathering caused by water that comes down from the surface or by water from underground streams.

Kinds of Soils

Modern soil scientists list 11 main groups of soils. These groups include more than 2,000 kinds of soils. To understand what soil scientists look for when describing soils, let us see what a few of the main groups include.

The *chernozem*, or *mollisols*, are chestnut-colored prairie soils. Their topsoils are rich in de-

Plants

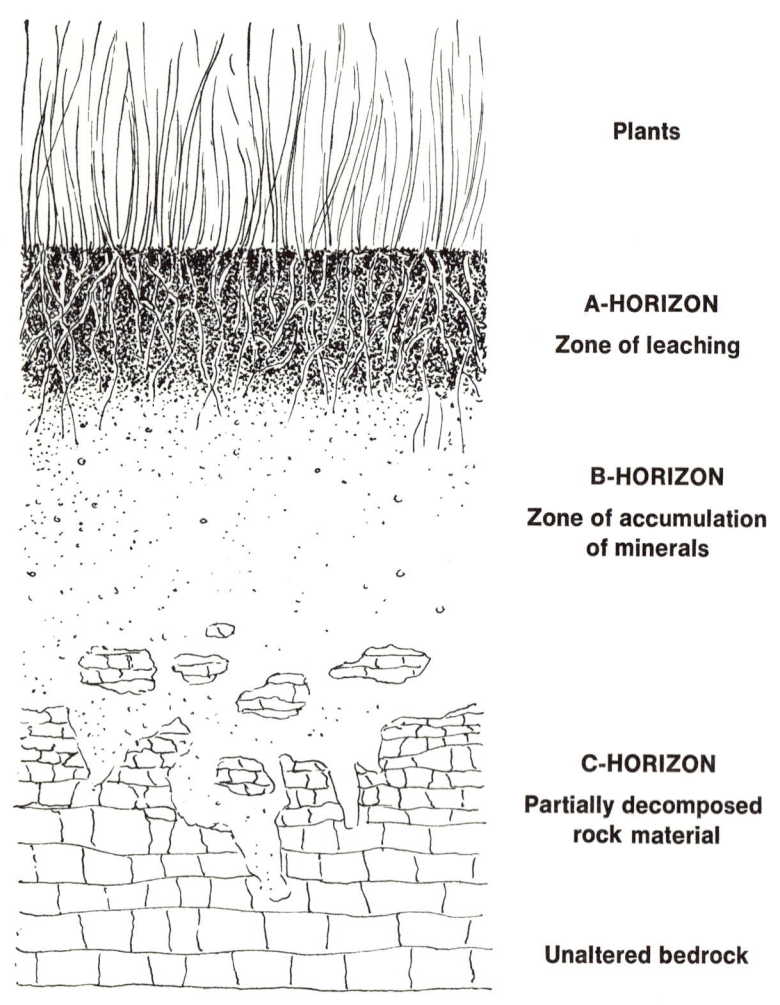

A-HORIZON
Zone of leaching

B-HORIZON
Zone of accumulation of minerals

C-HORIZON
Partially decomposed rock material

Unaltered bedrock

Profile of a prairie soil, a chernozem, or mollisol.

cayed materials, which come from grass. Chernozem are very good for growing crops. The prairie soils of the United States are chernozems.

Podzols, or *spodosols*, are brown forest soils that form in places where the climate is moist and temperate. The evergreen needles and other tree leaves make such thick layers that decay is not complete. The topsoil lacks some minerals that crop plants need, so podzols are not rich farm soils. Podzols cover much of the eastern half of the United States.

Desert soils, or *aridisols*, have much lime and other minerals near the surface. These soils are so dry that plants usually cannot grow in them. Therefore, desert soils have very little decayed materials, which keeps them light-colored and sandy.

What Kind of Soil Where?

Early soil scientists believed that the kind of soil in an area depends on the kind of bedrock that is weathering in the C-horizon. For example, weathered granite would form one kind of soil, and weathered limestone another kind. These scientists were not right, but they were not entirely wrong either. Soil *does* depend partly on the bedrock materials from which it forms. In some areas, you can even make a map of the bedrock by seeing the kinds of soils that cover them. But as soil scientists learned more and more, they realized that the make-up of soil depended on other things besides the kind of rock from which it came.

One of these things is the shape of the land. The soil at the top of a hill is different from the soil on the slope or at the bottom. This is because minerals that weather out of rock on the upper parts of a hill are carried downhill by rainwater. Soil at the top of a hill lacks minerals that accumulate at the bottom.

Another thing on which kinds of soils depend is climate — the long-time average temperature and rainfall — of an area. For instance, in the eastern half of the United States, the climate is usually mild and moist. Forests grow well in this climate, so the soils are generally of the podzol type. The climate of the prairie states of the United States is mostly dry, with hot summers. Grass grows well there, and the soils are chernozems.

We have seen that soil is made up of tiny pieces of rock and bits of decaying plants and animals. And we have seen how these soil particles make up horizons and different kinds of soil. But there is still another very important part of soil — the living part.

5

THE LIVING SOIL—
I. Animals

A great many different kinds of animals live in soil. They range in size from foot-long mammals, to insects, to one-celled animals that you need a microscope to see. The soil is also full of roots, seeds, and microscopically small plants. The numbers of these living things are so vast, and their bulk makes up so large a part of soil, that we cannot accurately speak of soil without including its living things. It is not just that the living things dwell *in* the soil, but that they make up an important part of soil.

Soil Mammals

The largest soil dwellers are mammals. Moles, shrews, mice, gophers, and prairie dogs are some mammals that spend all, or most, of their time within soil. Moles, for example, spend their whole lives within the soil. These six-inch animals almost never come out. They tunnel back and forth, an inch or two below the surface, as they search for worms and insects to eat.

Shrews spend almost as much time underground as do moles. But they do see the light of day now and then as they dash from one network of tunnels into another. Unlike moles and shrews, mice spend much of their time scurrying about aboveground. But they are important soil animals because of the seeds and other plant materials they take into their underground burrows. These materials eventually decay and become part of the soil. Air is needed by the living part of soil, and tunnels and burrows let air into soil.

Insects

Although mammals play a part in the making of soil, the most important soil animals are insects and other very small creatures.

There are more than a million kinds of insects, and most of them spend at least part of their lives in the soil. Some may be living within buried eggs from which they will hatch. Others may move through the soil as larvae feeding hungrily on plant roots, on other larvas, or on smaller animals. Insects may lie dormant for years in the soil as pupae waiting to emerge as fully developed insects. Or they may be burrowing insects that live all their lives within soil.

There are many other soil animals that we usually think of as insects, but really are not. Among these are earthworms, sowbugs, centipedes, millipedes, spiders, and mites. One naturalist made a rough count of the insects and insectlike animals in only half a square foot of soil. He found

15 ants	3 centipedes
4 beetles	10 millipedes
15 springtails	1 spider
8 aphids	32 fly pupae
4 wireworms	23 mites
4 earthworms	1 Japanese beetle pupa
6 sowbugs	22 others

This is a total of 158 in just one spadeful. In one acre, it amounts to nearly 14 million insects and insectlike soil animals. But this number includes only those at the depth of a spade, and insects live several feet deep in the soil.

Searching through a small piece of soil can be a surprising activity. (If you live in a city, dig soil from an empty lot. Don't dig up the soil in a park. Parks are for everyone and must not be damaged in any way.)

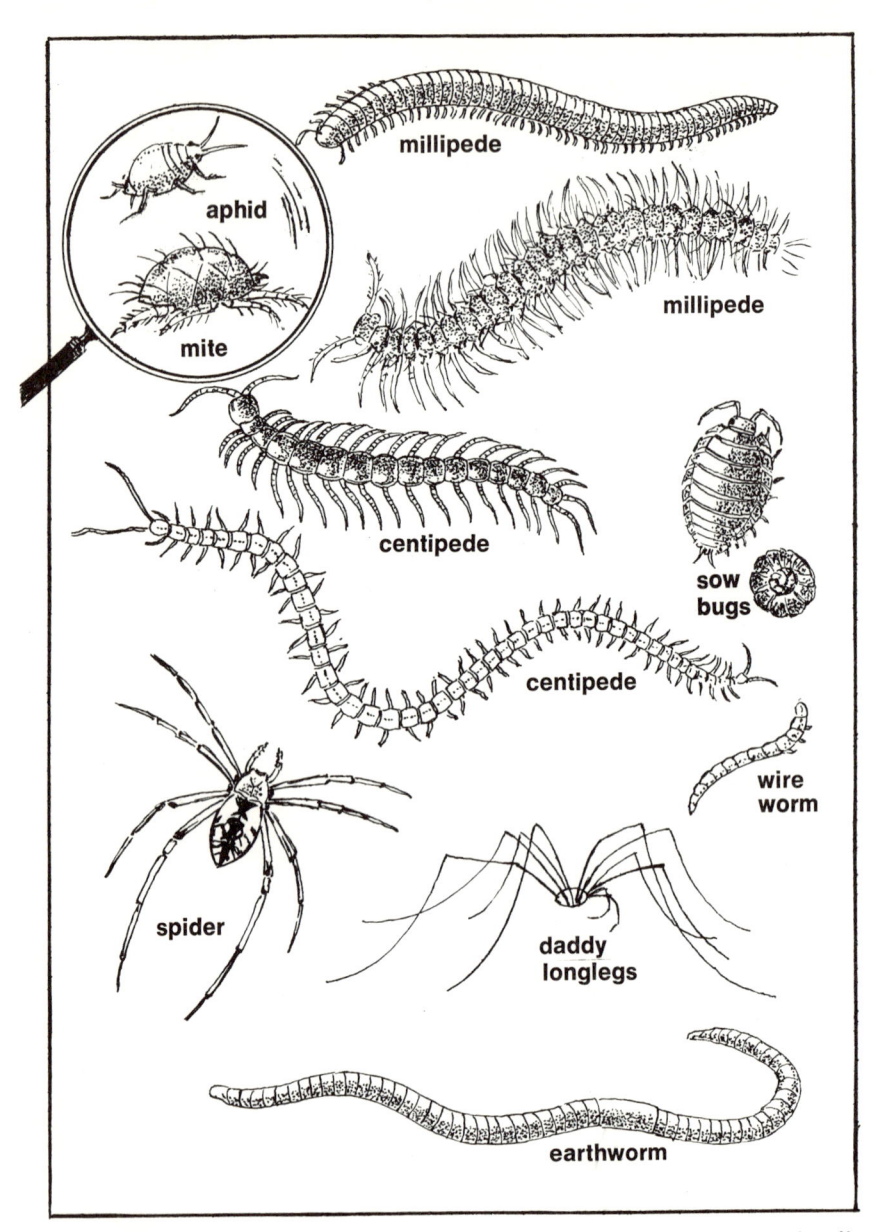

Some insectlike soil animals you may find in your bag of soil.

Get a 1-foot-square piece of cloth. If the piece is not square, it will not matter as long as it is about the same size. What is important is that the cloth have only very small openings between the woven threads. Bedsheets are made of this kind of cloth.

Measure a 4-inch-square on the ground. Dig up this square of soil, pushing your spade no more than 3 inches deep. Put the soil on the cloth. Gather the edges of the cloth together to make a bag. Using string, tie the bag closed very tightly, so that no small insect can crawl out. Hang the bag up where the sun will shine on it and breezes can blow around it. This is done to dry the soil. As it dries, squeeze the soil a few times to break up clods.

At the end of three days, dump the dried soil on a large sheet of white paper. Using a penknife or a sharp-pointed stick, pick the soil apart. Count the living and dead insects and insectlike animals. Look sharp, and be quick to catch those that crawl away. Keep a record of the number of each kind. When you have picked through the whole mound of soil, multiply the total number by 9. A 4-inch square contains 16 square inches, which equals 1/9 square foot. So, when you multiply by 9, you will find the number of soil animals in 1 square foot of your soil.

Earthworms

Earthworms are especially important soil animals because the great number of holes they tunnel in the soil let in air and water. And their feeding activities make soil much richer for growing plants. They eat pieces of decaying leaves and blades of grass which they pull into their burrows. Some earthworms eat soil, taking nourishment from the tiny bits of decaying materials in it. Then, in their bodies, the decayed materials and soil are ground very fine and are left behind as wastes. Scientists have estimated that there may be as many as a million earthworms in an acre of soil. The earthworms pass as much as 36 tons through their bodies in one year.

Mites

These insectlike animals belong to the same group as spiders. Although they spend part of their lives above ground, you usually cannot see them. Most kinds are so small that you would need a powerful magnifying glass to do so.

Some mites, such as chiggers and ticks, are parasites that feed on body fluids of animals, including people. They attach themselves to the body, feed, and then drop off.

Other mites are parasites on soil mammals and insects. Still other mites eat microscopically small soil animals, or feed on decaying plant and animal wastes. Mites can damage crops by sucking the juices from plant roots.

Nematodes, or Threadworms

Wriggling through the spaces between soil particles of almost every square inch of soil are huge numbers of small eel-like animals called nematodes. These creatures are so small that if you lined them up end to end, it would take 50 of them to make one inch; and placed side-by-side, it would take 1,000. Their bodies are round, and they are also called roundworms or threadworms.

The smallest nematodes eat bacteria in the soil. Larger ones eat other nematodes. However, many of them spend at least part of their lives as parasites in either plants or animals, usually causing disease. In soil, nematodes suck juices from plant roots, taking the plants' nourishment, thus killing them. More than 100,000,000,000 nematodes may be found in an acre of soil. As a result, they do hundreds of millions of dollars' worth of damage to crops.

Protozoa

Protozoa are the smallest of all animals. Each is a single cell, and the largest kinds are only about 1/10 of an inch long. They ooze along and swim through the water that is found on and between soil grains. The two main kinds of protozoa found in soil are *amebas* and *flagellates.* An acre of soil may have 1,000,000 protozoa swimming and oozing along in the water on and in between soil grains. Protozoa that live in soil feed on bacteria and do little harm or good to the soil or to man.

The vast numbers of animals found in an acre of soil prove that you must include living things when you think of soil.

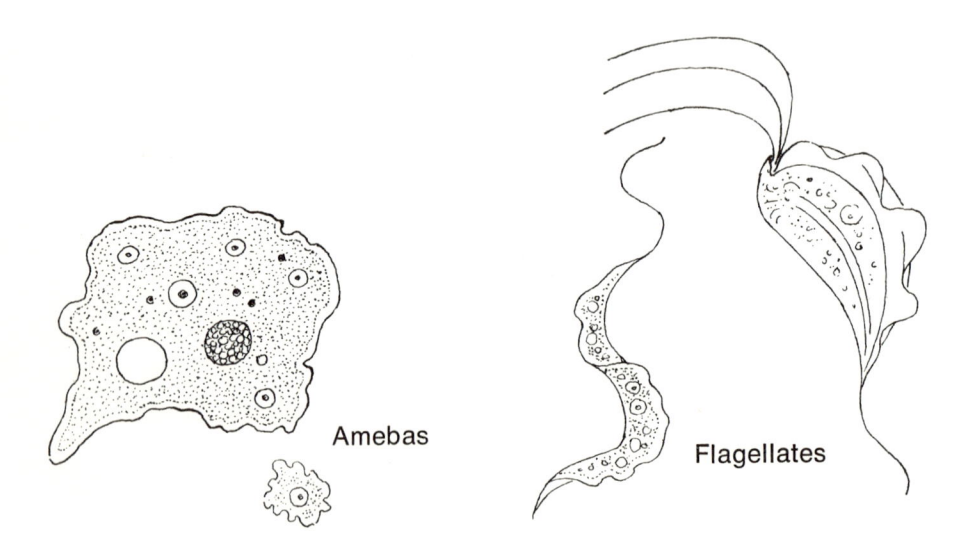

Amebas

Flagellates

6

THE LIVING SOIL—
II. Plants

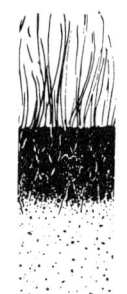

The other living part of the soil consists of plants. Some float in water, some grow high in trees, and some grow on bare rocks; but most plants grow in soil. The parts of growing plants that you see are stems and leaves, flowers and fruits. You cannot see the largest parts of most plants because they are underground. These parts are the *roots.*

When a plant seed germinates, or sprouts, the first thing that appears from inside the seed coat is a tiny root. It grows down into the soil, from which it takes water and the minerals dissolved in the water. The root not only becomes the largest part of the plant, but also may make up a large part of the soil in which it grows. To see just how much of the bulk of soil can be roots, cut a small piece of grassy soil out of a lawn, digging down about five inches. Then soak the piece of turf in water, swishing it around until all the soil has been washed out. Or, turn the sod upside down and direct a strong stream of water from a hose upon it. The thick matted mass that remains is the roots of the grass. One naturalist measured the roots grown by a rye grass plant only four months old. He found *7,000 miles* of roots!

Fungi

    Fungi, you remember, are plants that cannot make their own food, as green plants can. Fungi are different from green plants in other ways, too. One is that fungi have no roots. Instead, they grow a network of fine threads which is called a *mycelium.* The mycelium is almost the whole fungus plant. A piece of mycelium that can fit into a saucer is made up of *miles* of threads. Since a fungus has no need for sunlight, it does not send stems and leaves up from the soil. Instead, the mycelium grows entirely within the soil. One kind of fungus you may have seen is bread mold. If you pick a piece of it apart with a pin, and look at the mold through a strong magnifying glass, you can see the fuzzy, stringy mycelium growing down into the bread.

    Many fungi are harmful to man and other animals, and there are a large number of fungus diseases that kill crops and other useful plants. As

Bread mold, a fungus.

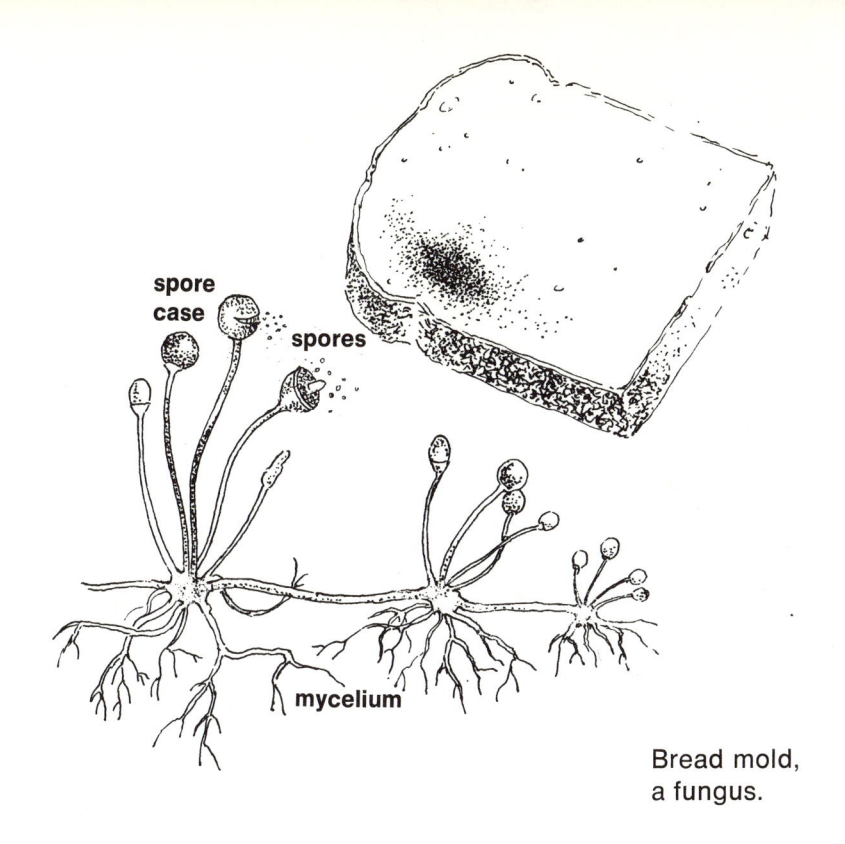

many as five million fungi may live in a teaspoonful of soil.

Actinomycetes

If you have ever been in a field when it was being plowed, you probably smelled the "earth" the plow was turning over. What you actually smelled were millions of very small plants called *actinomycetes*, which the plow had uncovered.

Actinomycetes are a link between fungi and

45

the smallest of all plants — bacteria. Although they look and grow like mold fungi, actinomycetes are as small as some kinds of bacteria.

Actinomycetes play a large part in the process of decay. They decompose dead plants and animals, breaking up the once-living matter into carbon and nitrogen. Putting carbon and nitrogen into the soil is one way in which actinomycetes are useful to man. They are also very valuable as the source of some of the powerful germ-killing medicines called *antibiotics.* Actinomycin and terramycin are the names of two antibiotics that come from actinomycetes.

Bacteria

There are thousands of different kinds of bacteria found everywhere on earth — in water, air, and soil. You cannot see bacteria without a microscope. Some are so small that you could put a million of them into this letter o.

Like fungi, bacteria are plants that cannot make their own food. To get food, they live in or on the bodies of other plants or animals, including people.

Bacteria in Soil

There are more bacteria in soil than all other

kinds of living things put together. You could find five billion bacteria in a teaspoonful of some kinds of soils. Bacteria are valuable in breaking down dead plants and animals into soil particles and chemical substances. If bacteria (and fungi and actinomycetes) did not do so, every inch of the surface of the earth would long ago have become covered with dead things. And life would have ended.

Nitrogen-Fixing Bacteria

Nitrogen is a chemical element. It is a gas that makes up four-fifths of the air. It is also part of all living things. Plants cannot grow without nitrogen, yet they cannot take it from the air. The nitrogen must first combine with other chemical elements and form substances that can dissolve in water. Then, plant roots take this water from the soil, and the plants have the nitrogen they need.

How does nitrogen from the air combine with other elements and get into the soil? This task is performed by *nitrogen-fixing bacteria* which live on the roots of a kind of plant called a *legume.* Alfalfa, peanuts, clover, and soybeans are examples of legumes. The bacteria live in groups that make *nodules*, or lumps, on the roots. Nitrogen-fixing bacteria take in nitrogen from the air that circulates between particles of soil. The bacteria use

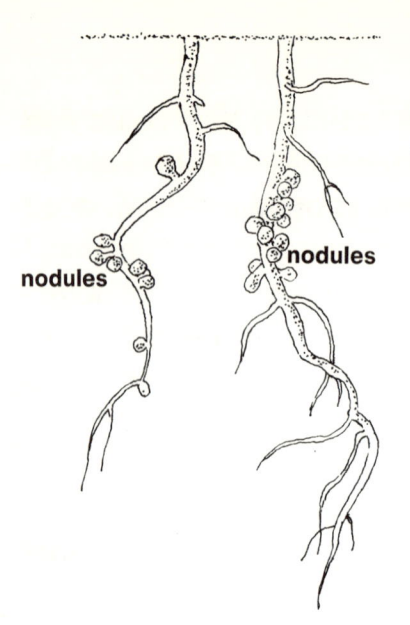

Nodules on the roots of soybean, a legume.

nodules

nodules

the nitrogen to make *protein* within their bodies. Protein is another substance that is part of all living things. When the legume dies, most of the bacteria die, too, and decay. This puts into the soil nitrogen-containing substances which other plants then are able to use.

Another way in which plants get nitrogen is through animals. Animals eat plants, and plant protein becomes animal protein. When plants and animals die, decay bacteria and fungi break down the proteins into nitrogen-containing substances called *nitrates.* Some nitrates dissolve in rainwater, and growing plants take them up from the soil.

Other kinds of soil bacteria, called *denitrifying*

bacteria, break up nitrates. In doing this, they release pure nitrogen gas, which goes back to the air. The round-and-round process through which nitrogen from air enters plants, then becomes part of the soil, and finally goes back to the air is called the *nitrogen cycle.*

The nitrogen cycle.

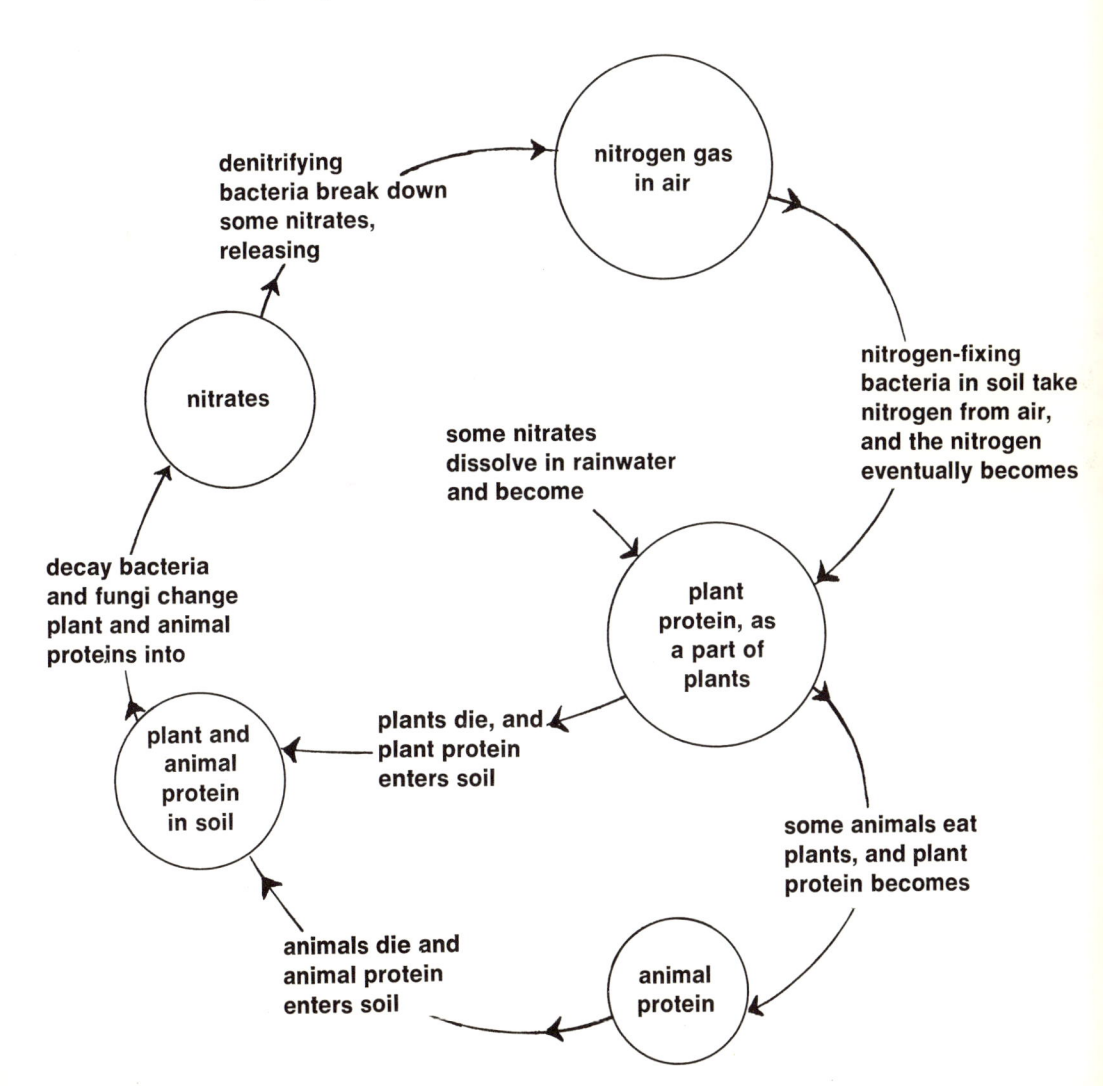

- nitrogen gas in air
- nitrogen-fixing bacteria in soil take nitrogen from air, and the nitrogen eventually becomes
- plant protein, as a part of plants
- some nitrates dissolve in rainwater and become
- some animals eat plants, and plant protein becomes
- animal protein
- animals die and animal protein enters soil
- plants die, and plant protein enters soil
- plant and animal protein in soil
- decay bacteria and fungi change plant and animal proteins into
- nitrates
- denitrifying bacteria break down some nitrates, releasing

Seeds

Seeds are living parts of plants. By making seeds, a plant reproduces — makes other plants like itself. A seed is a tiny plant surrounded by its seed coat, which is a tough protective coating. When a seed is in proper conditions of temperature, moisture, and air — conditions it usually finds

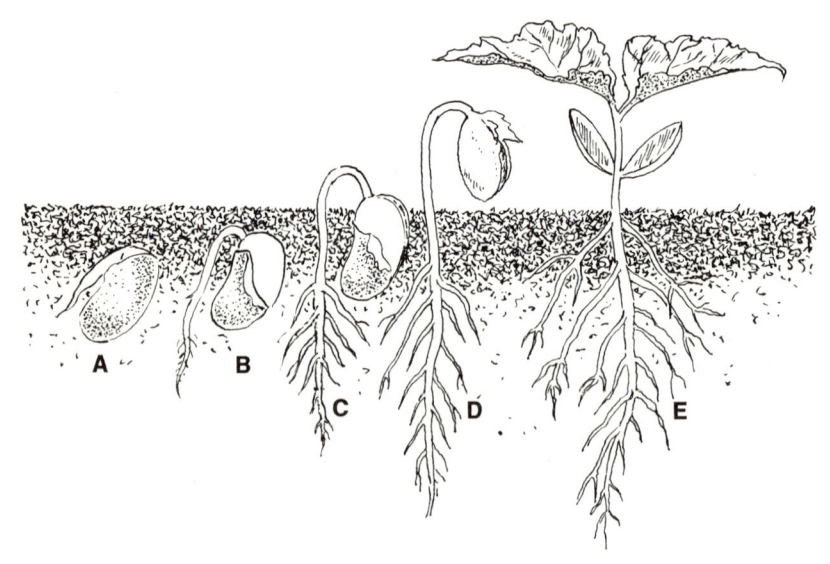

Seed Germinating, or Sprouting
  A. Root pushes out of split seed coat and turns downward.
  B. Seed coat splits further, and root hairs appear on root.
  C. Upper part of root pushes out of soil and begins to pull up rest of seed.
  D. Upper part of root becomes stem, and first leaves appear.
  E. Leaves expand to catch sunlight, and plant begins to make its own food.

in soil — the seed coat splits, and the tiny plant begins to grow into a plant like the one that made the seed. Seeds are considered a part of soil because there are so many of them.

For hundreds of millions of years, soil-making processes — weathering, decay, and the activities of soil animals — increased the amount of soil. Today, the opposite is true. The earth is losing soil. Let us see how this has happened.

7
THE WAR FOR SOIL

There have been human beings for more than a million years. For almost all of that time, people got their food by hunting, fishing, and searching for fruits, berries, nuts, and roots.

About 10,000 or 12,000 years ago, men learned to grow food crops and herd cattle. Farming provided people with enough food so they could store some for winter. They no longer had to hunt animals for meat, or wander south in winter and north in summer, looking for food plants. Farming people also harvested and stored enough grass to feed cattle during the winter. Then the herding people no longer had to drive their herds south in winter and north in summer, seeking grass for their cattle. Thanks to stored food, farmers and herdsmen could remain in one place all year long. Now they could build permanent settlements, towns and cities.

War Begins

The first people who settled down to grow food crops began a war for good soil. Until only a short time ago, man lost almost every battle in his war with soil. And almost every battle was lost in the same way. Let us see how this happened to one ancient nation.

In the country that is now Iraq, wind-blown sand has buried the remains of several ancient civilizations. One such civilization was the large and powerful nation of Babylonia.

Each year, there was a rainy season. During

These are the ruins of the great city of Kish, which lost its battle for soil 6,000 years ago.

the rest of the year, rain was scarce and the soil was dry. But Babylonia was located between two large rivers — the Tigris and the Euphrates — and its people learned how to use these rivers to make up for the lack of rain. Engineers dug long, deep canals and lined them with bricks. They let water from the rivers run through the canals to the crop fields, miles from the rivers. Finally, the water flowed into furrows — long, narrow trenches made by plows — between the rows of crops. This way of bringing water to crops is called *irrigation.*

Worn-Out Soil

By irrigating the land, the farmers of Babylonia could grow crop after crop in the same soil. When the crops were harvested, all parts of the plants except the roots were taken from the fields. This left very little plant material to decay, and return to the soil some of the substances containing nitrogen and minerals which the growing crops used.

As crop after crop was harvested, there were less and less minerals and nitrogen left in the soil. Each crop became smaller, the plants did not grow as thickly and as tall, and each plant bore less and less grain and other kinds of fruits. Farmers said that their soil had become "worn out." They did not know why. (We now know that the crops had taken so much nitrogen and minerals out of the soil that the plants could not get these things, which they must have to grow.) A Babylonian farmer with worn-out soil had to find new land for planting crops. After a number of years, the new land, too, became unfit for growing crops.

Losing Soil

Farmers also planted their crops in straight rows, and kept the furrows between the rows clear of weeds. During the rainy season, water ran swiftly along the furrows, washing away soil. The loss of soil was especially bad when the furrows were plowed straight uphill and downhill. Then the rainwater raced even more swiftly through the furrows and scoured out deep channels here and there. Being the lowest places in a field, these channels carried the most water. This cut the channels deeper and deeper. The sides of the deep channels kept caving in, making them wider and wider. Eventually, these channels became deep gullies which reached down into the subsoil, to the B-horizon, and even to the C-horizon. Whole fields were destroyed by the spread of gullies. The action of water in changing the surface of the earth is called *water erosion*, or usually just *erosion*.

Further erosion was caused as the population of Babylonia grew and more and more houses and temples had to be built. For lumber, whole forests were cut from the mountainsides. Bricks used in building were made by baking clay, and firewood was needed for the fires. This meant that more trees had to be cut. But, as trees were cut from the hills and mountains, rainwater washed the soil down to the valleys. Then, during the dry seasons, wind blew the topsoil off the bare, treeless hills and mountainsides. Loss of soil in this way is called *wind erosion.*

The people in the growing cities of Babylonia needed meat, milk, and wool. Herdsmen pastured their cattle in grassy fields, and shepherds took their sheep and goats into the hills to graze.

Blades of grass are the leaves of the grass plant. The process by which the grass plant makes its food takes place in them. Blades of grass are cut down or torn out of the soil by grazing animals. The short blades must be allowed to grow long and new blades to form before grazing animals are allowed to feed on the same pasture land again. If not, the grass plant will not be able to make any food and it will starve.

The Babylonians' demands for meat, milk, and wool were so great that the shepherds and herdsmen drove their animals to graze too often on the same grass. The grass starved, and the pastures eventually became bare of grass. Then the rains washed the bare soil away.

The soil that washed or blew off the fields and hills filled the irrigation canals with mud. The mud had to be dug out. As the soil was washed off more and more poorly farmed and overgrazed land, it became harder and harder to clean the canals. Thousands of Babylonians had to work at this task, but they were not enough. Prisoners of war were put to work digging mud out of the

These students are looking at an irrigation canal filled with soil stripped from fields by erosion in the same way as in Babylonia.

canals. They, too, were not enough. Canals had to be abandoned and new canals built to carry water to new farmland. Eventually, they too filled with mud.

At last, after centuries of struggle, the task of clearing the canals became too much for the Babylonians. The amount of land they could farm became less and less. The land fed fewer and fewer people and cattle. The population lessened. People left the big cities. The great nation of Babylonia became a land of small farming villages and a few trading towns.

Assyria, Persia, India, Greece, and Rome all lost their battles with soil in the same ways as Babylonia — although the exact way each nation lost was a little different from that of the others.

The American Way

Today, the United States grows more food crops than any other country, and its citizens are the best fed of all the people in the world. Knowing this, you might guess that the people who settled in the United States and the farmers who followed have used the soil wisely. But is this true?

When the first settlers arrived, they found the land east of the Allegheny Mountains covered almost completely by a huge forest. The land was

The owner of this Texas farm grew cotton and corn without doing anything to protect his soil. Erosion took away all his topsoil and scarred his farm with gullies (the light-colored areas).

free or very cheap. The settlers immediately set about cutting down that forest. They used some trees for lumber, but mostly they cleared the land for farming. They planted crop after crop in the same soil. When they no longer could grow crops in that soil, they cut down more trees and plowed up the soil. They plowed straight furrows up and down the hills of the Alleghenies, and rainwater washed the soil away and scarred the land with big gullies.

When there was no more good land nearby,

a farmer sold his house and land for whatever he could get. He bought a big wagon, and put in it all the possessions he could carry. He tied his plow, shovels, and hoes to the outside of the wagon. Then he and his family joined the new settlers on their way to Ohio, Indiana, and Illinois, and out upon the sea of grass and deep rich soil — the prairies. There was more than enough land to be had in the West. In the 1850s, land on the prairie cost only $1.25 an acre.

Finally, about 80 years ago, no more good land was left. But settlers kept coming. They farmed land on which the topsoil was thin, and they destroyed it in a few years.

Of course, not all the early farmers were so careless. If they had been, we would not have any soil now. Many worked their farms carefully. There are farms in New Jersey that were first planted around 1650 by Dutch settlers, and the soil on these farms is still producing good crops. And in other parts of the country, too, good crops are being grown on the same farms where the settlers' plows first turned the soil. Nevertheless, the record of the way soil in the United States was used is a shameful one.

Soil experts have found that in the crop-growing areas of the United States, half the soil is

This was a farm before rainwater erosion stripped away all the unprotected topsoil. No crops can be grown in this field now.

damaged. Two hundred and fifty million acres are seriously damaged by rainwater. Thirty-five million acres of farmland have been abandoned as worthless because crops can no longer be grown on them. One hundred million acres of former farmland are now used to grow grass and trees, because they were so badly damaged that it would cost too much to grow crops on them. Another 100 million acres have been damaged by wind, and

10 million of these must be abandoned. We are losing half a million acres of soil each year to the action of rainwater.

Although we are far from the trouble in which the Babylonians put themselves, we have a growing population and our need for food and other crops will increase. We not only must stop our losses of topsoil, but must find ways to reclaim soil in the areas where it has been almost — but not entirely — destroyed by careless farming.

8
SOIL SCIENCE

In ancient times, as one generation of farmers followed another, men began to learn things about soil and how to use it best. This knowledge accumulated slowly. Then, in the 1600s, *soil science*, or *pedology*, began. Since that time, pedologists have found ways to improve soil, conserve it, and grow large crops in it.

Crop Field, Fallow Field

Babylonian farmers discovered that after a field of worn-out soil had been abandoned for a number of years, crops could be grown in it again. This was because weeds had grown in the worn-out soil. The weeds died and decayed. In a few years, some of the minerals and nitrogen had been returned to the soil by the decaying weed plants. The soil was not as good as new, but some crops could be grown in it.

Later, Greek and Roman farmers made use of what the Babylonians had learned about abandoned fields. But the Greeks and Romans did not wait until soil became completely worn out. Instead, they planted crops in one field and left the neighboring field unplanted, or *fallow.* At the end of the summer, they plowed the fallow field and turned the weeds into the soil. This quickened the decay of the weeds. The next spring, they planted crops in the field that had been fallow, and they let the other field lie fallow. Changing from crop field to fallow field, year after year, increased the number of years good crops could be grown in a field.

European farmers of the Middle Ages improved on two-field farming. They used three fields. They had noticed that when certain crops were harvested and the plant roots were plowed into the earth, the soil became especially good for the next planting. The crops were peas and certain beans. These are legumes, the plants that have on their roots bacteria which bring nitrogen from the air to the soil. So, European farmers planted one field in crops, such as wheat, barley, or vegetables. A second field was planted in peas or beans. A third was allowed to lie fallow. The next year, the field

wheat barley vegetables
peas beans
fallow

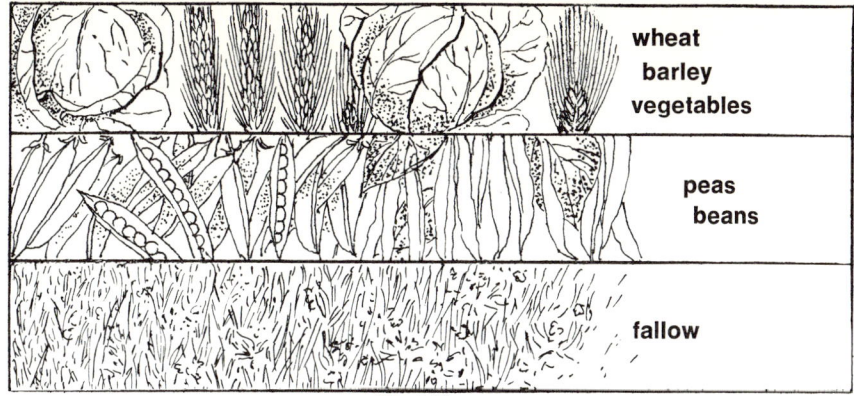

First Year

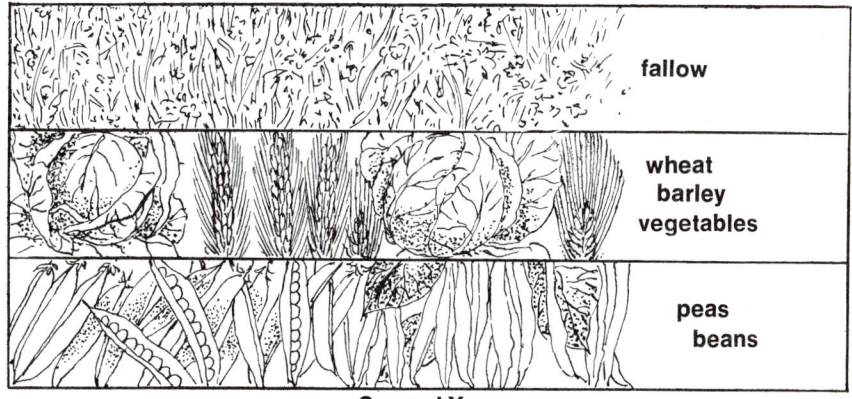

fallow
wheat barley vegetables
peas beans

Second Year

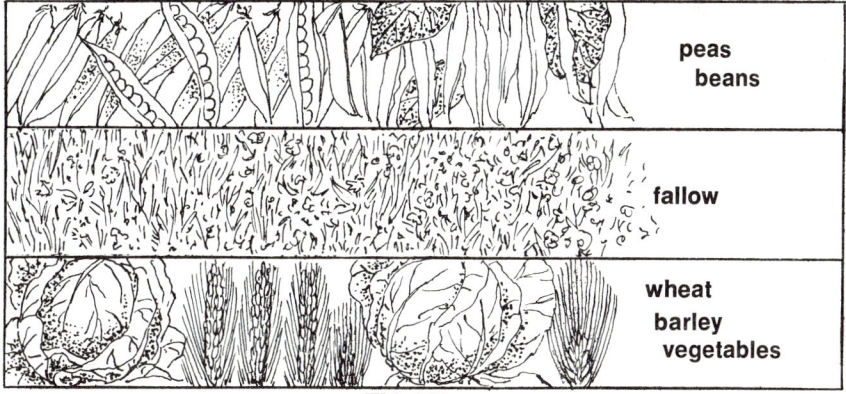

peas beans
fallow
wheat barley vegetables

Third Year

Three-field farming.

that had legumes was planted with other crops. The fallow field was planted with peas or beans. And the field that had crops the previous summer was allowed to lie fallow. The three-field way of planting is called *crop rotation.* In modern crop rotation, only two fields are used; there usually is no fallow field.

Fertilizer

Even before the time of Babylonia, farmers found that they could grow good crops year after year in the same soil by putting horse, cattle, and sheep manure on their fields. Putting any material, such as manure, on soil is *fertilizing* the soil, and the material is *fertilizer.* The animals' waste materials contain nitrogen and minerals that plants need. But the farmers did not have enough manure to put on all of their soil.

Then, farmers learned of another natural material that could be used to fertilize soil. This plant material, or mulch, consisted of partly decayed plant matter, such as straw, cut grass, dead leaves, and other parts of plants. It is made by piling up dead plant materials and letting them partly decay. Then the mulch is spread on fields and plowed into the soil.

In 1908, Fritz Haber, a German chemist, found a way to combine nitrogen from air with hydrogen gas. This formed ammonia, which could easily be used to make chemical substances called *nitrates.* These are the same substances that are formed by the decay of dead bacteria on the roots of legumes. Nitrates dissolve in water. Roots then take in nitrates, and the plants get the nitrogen they need. Haber's discovery was a giant step forward for agriculture.

As soil scientists learned which minerals plants need, chemists learned to make them. The two most important minerals contain *phosphorus* and *potassium.* These are combined with oxygen to form substances that will dissolve in water. Nine other chemical elements are needed, in smaller amounts. Finally, a few more are needed in only very small amounts, or traces. All these chemical substances can be mixed together into a single fertilizer that gives plants all the things they need to grow and produce fruit.

Chemical fertilizer can greatly increase the crops grown in poor soil. For example, almost all the soil of India is badly damaged, and most of the Indian people have lived with less food than they have needed. Millions have starved. Now the

Indian government provides farmers with chemical fertilizer which makes the poor soil yield almost enough food for all the people of India.

There is, however, a bad side to the use of chemical fertilizer. Some farmers with good soil use large amounts of chemical fertilizer to grow greatly increased crops. This works for a few years, but eventually it kills the living part of the soil. Then the farmer gets fewer and fewer crops from his overfertilized, damaged soil. Too much fertilizer damages soil as surely as erosion does.

Another disadvantage is that the nitrogen in chemical fertilizer can poison crops grown in overfertilized soil. Eating such crops makes many people sick, and actually kills a number of babies in the United States each year.

However, chemical fertilizer can be good if just enough is used to replace the nitrogen and other chemical elements taken out of the soil by growing crops. Forcing large crops from soil by using large amounts of fertilizer can be worse than using none at all.

Wind Erosion

When weather is dry for several weeks or more, soil in which no plants are growing will be lost to erosion by wind. This happened in Babylonia, and since then it has happened in thousands of other places.

In the 1930s, the United States had a very serious wind erosion problem in a large area that

This is a dust storm roaring into Perryton, Texas, on April 14, 1935.

was called the Dust Bowl. It covered the states of Kansas, Oklahoma, Texas, New Mexico, and Colorado.

From 1918, when World War I ended, until the 1930s both the United States and Europe needed large amounts of corn, wheat, and meat. Farmers plowed and planted every acre of soil they could, because they knew they would sell all the crops they grew. Cattlemen grazed their herds until pasture land was overgrazed. Then, at the beginning of the 1930s, great numbers of people all over the United States and Europe lost their jobs and could buy very little food. The demand for grain and meat fell sharply. Farmers and cattle raisers found they could not sell their grain and cattle. Since they could make no money, they had to go elsewhere to earn a living. They left unplanted fields and overgrazed pasture land behind them.

At the same time, a *drought* left the soil powdery dry. With no growing plants to protect it from the wind, much of the soil was blown into the air. Huge dust storms moved across the area. In places as far away as New York, dust dimmed the sun. Millions of tons of topsoil blew out of the Dust Bowl. Soil particles from the region covered the President's desk in Washington.

In 1938, the drought finally ended. Dust Bowl farmers tried to grow crops in the soil that remained. With the help of soil scientists, they planted quick-growing grass to protect the soil from the wind. Then they planted lines of trees to act as *windbreaks.* These trees slowed the wind, making it drop most of the soil particles it carried. In the autumn, the grass was plowed into the earth and crops were planted in its place.

Today, the former Dust Bowl is a fertile farming and grazing area. There have been droughts in this area since the one in the 1930s, but the plant-covered soil has held against wind erosion.

Although wind erosion has destroyed much soil throughout the history of farming, the main destroyer of soil has been rainwater erosion. One reason for this is that, until only a short time ago, no one understood exactly how rainwater did its damage.

9
RAINDROPS ARE BOMBS

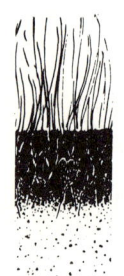

Even before the time of Babylonia, farmers knew that rainwater carried away soil. But in all the thousands of years that this fact was known, no one really understood how the water did its damage. It seemed that rainwater flowing over bare soil simply loosened the soil and carried it away. They called this action *sheet erosion*, because one rain after another carried off layer after layer of soil, like taking sheets of paper off a pile.

It is easy to see how this idea arose. The fast-moving streams of rainwater could actually be seen tearing pieces of earth off the sides and bottoms of gullies. So it seemed that rainwater flowing over the surface of bare land tore up tiny bits of soil and carried them away.

Only about 25 years ago, soil scientists found the real cause of soil erosion — raindrops. No one

If nothing is done about this gully, it will grow much bigger, and all the soil of this field will be washed away.

had paid attention to them. Each one seemed so small and harmless.

However, raindrops act like bombs. When a raindrop strikes bare soil, it first makes a small dent, or crater. Then the raindrop bursts, flinging water outward on all sides. This water carries with it the soil from the sides of the tiny crater. The soil is flung into the thin sheet of rainwater that is

Three raindrops — two of them close together — blasting unprotected soil. The bared pebbles show that the rain is eroding away the soil. The very muddy water shows that soil particles have been loosened and will be carried away by the flowing rainwater.

flowing over the surface of the ground, and the soil is carried away. If raindrops did not blast soil loose, water flowing over the bare ground would carry away about only one-tenth of the soil that it actually does.

Once particles of soil have been blasted loose, and are in the flowing water, falling raindrops keep the water stirred up. This prevents the soil particles from settling out of the water to the ground, and the flowing rainwater can carry them long distances.

You can prove what soil scientists have learned about erosion. You will need two flat boards, some soil, a hose with a nozzle, and a watch. Make the soil into mud. Smear it on one side of each board, and let the mud dry.

Put the boards flat on the ground. Place stones under one end of each board, so that these raised ends are about an inch higher than the other ends. With the nozzle off the hose, turn on the water so that it just about flows out of the hose in a steady stream. Put the end of the hose on the raised end of one board. Let the water flow over the dried mud for half a minute. The water running out of the hose represents rainwater flowing over bare ground.

Put the nozzle on the end of the hose and regulate it so that water squirts out in a number of fine streams. Do *not* turn the water on any stronger than in the first part of this experiment. Direct the water up into the air, so that it falls like raindrops, and let the drops fall on the second board for half a minute. Can you explain why your "raindrops" washed off more mud than the flowing water did?

In the upper photograph, water flowing from the hose for half a minute has eroded away very little of the soil that was dried on a board. In the lower photograph, "raindrops" from the hose nozzle (arrow) have been falling for half a minute. See how parts of the board and pebbles have been bared by erosion due to the blasting action of the falling drops of water.

Ground Cover Protects

Soil scientists have known for a long time that erosion takes hardly any soil from land that has plants — grass, bushes, or trees — growing on it. For example:

Kind of Ground Cover	*Number of Years for Erosion to Remove Seven Inches of Soil from Level Ground*
None (bare ground)	18
Cotton (clean furrows)	46
Rotated crops	110
Grass	82,000
Forest	575,000

Scientists used to think that the roots of plants held the soil particles, and this kept sheet erosion from washing soil away. Roots *do* stop some erosion, by breaking up the flow of water over the ground. This slows down the water, and lets some soil particles settle to the ground.

But when scientists discovered the blasting action of raindrops, they changed their ex-

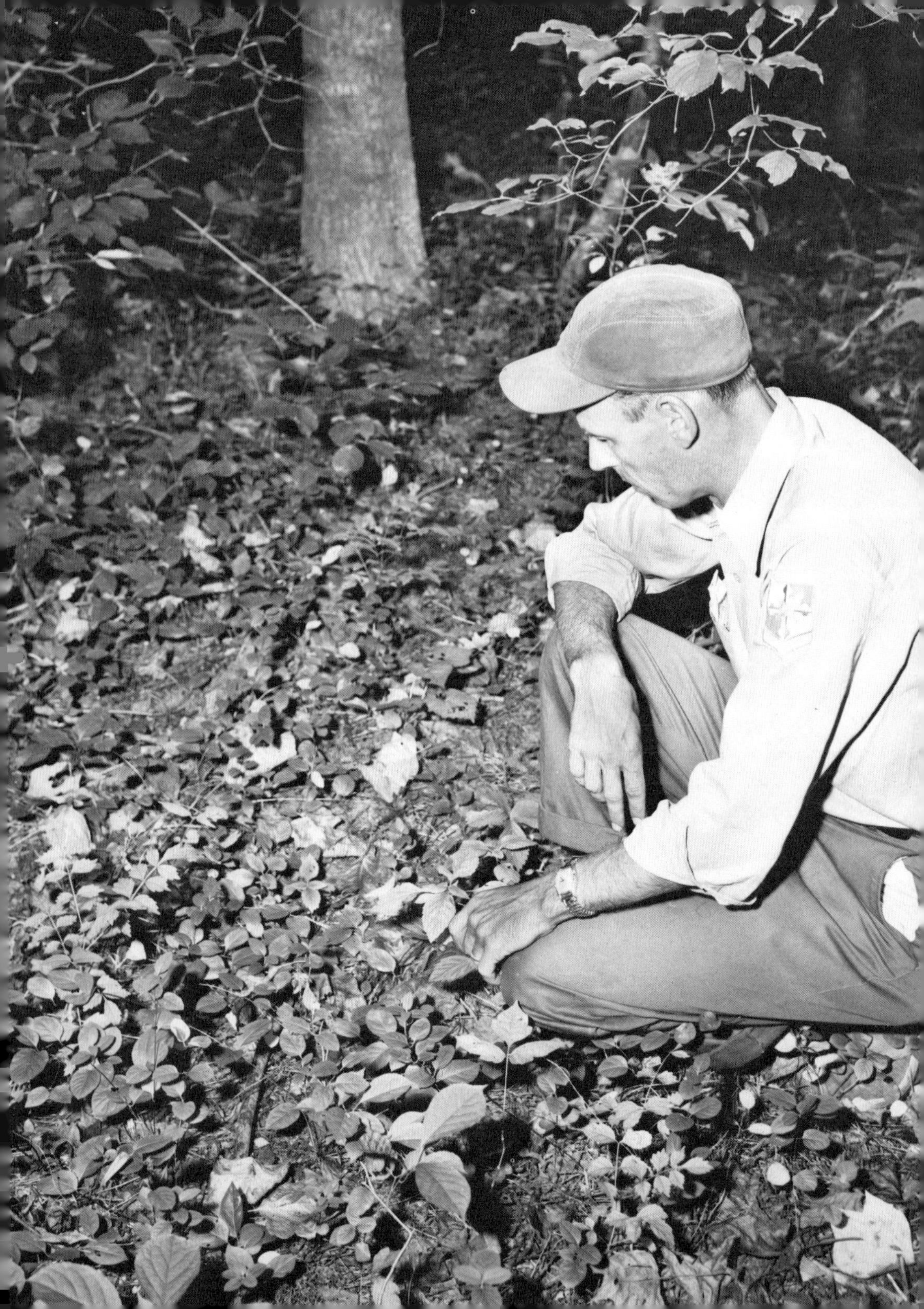

planation. They realized that the main reason plants hold back erosion is that they keep raindrops from hitting the ground. After falling on leaves or blades of grass, raindrops drip to the ground or trickle down branches and stems. A drop of water falling to the ground from a blade of grass or a leaf on a bush lacks enough energy to blast soil loose.

Go back to your boards. Again smear them with mud and let it dry. This time, after you have propped up one end of each board, cover one with a one-inch-thick layer of straw, cut grass, or leaves. Now let "raindrops" from the hose fall on each board in turn. Why did the covered board keep its mud so much longer?

More Raindrop Damage

There are other ways in which raindrops destroy soil. Good soil contains a large amount of decaying plant and animal materials. Most of these materials float in water, and they are the first to be carried away by flowing water, when raindrops splash into unprotected soil.

The plants on the floor of this forest make up a living cover that prevents erosion of the soil by water dripping from the treetops.

Good soil is loose and crumbly. It is made up of clumps of soil particles, with spaces between the clumps and the particles themselves. The spaces allow air to circulate within the soil, and air is needed by the things that make up the living part of soil.

When soil is stirred up by raindrops, rainwater carries some of the smaller rock particles into the spaces in the soil. These spaces become filled with the small particles, which are called *silt*. With the spaces blocked by silt, the living things in soil cannot get the air they need. Also, rainwater cannot sink deep into the soil. Instead, the water runs over the surface of the ground, carrying away more soil.

To see the difference between good topsoil and the subsoil left after erosion has taken place, try this experiment. Find a place where there is crumbly, dark-colored topsoil. Dig up a small bagful and put it aside. Dig down through the topsoil to the subsoil, the B-horizon. Dig up a small bagful of subsoil. If you can find a place where erosion has washed away the topsoil and left subsoil exposed, dig up a bagful of this soil instead of digging down to subsoil. If you cannot find any erosion-bared soil, the subsoil will do quite well.

Take a handful of topsoil and squeeze it in your fist. Open your fingers and see how the crumbly topsoil falls apart in the palm of your hand. Squeeze a handful of the subsoil and open your fingers. See how the subsoil sticks together in big lumps.

Topsoil that has been squeezed in the left fist remains crumbly, while subsoil squeezed in the right fist sticks together in lumps.

The mound of subsoil, on the right, became so hard upon drying that it could be picked up and placed next to the crumbly mound of dried topsoil.

Take two flat containers such as pie plates or dessert dishes. In one put some topsoil, and in the other an equal amount of subsoil. Add just enough water to make thick mud. On a thick sheet of paper, spoon enough mud from each container to make a small pie. Allow the mud pies to dry thoroughly. This may take as long as two days. In the picture on page 82, see how the topsoil has crumbled, making a mound of separate pieces with air spaces between. The dried subsoil has become a single hard lump.

10
THE MODERN USE OF SOIL

A modern American farmer does not simply plant whatever crop he wants to grow. When he decides to plant on new land, he calls in a soil scientist. The soil expert probably is a member of the United States Soil Conservation Service or is from a state university or state agricultural extension service.

The soil scientist examines the land carefully. He finds out how many different kinds of soil make up the new farmland. He tests the soil to learn how acid or alkaline it is; whether it is sandy, clayey, or some mixture between; what kinds of rock materials are in the B-horizon; and other things. He also surveys the land to measure the steepness of any hills. When he has gathered all this information, he makes a *soil capability map.* This map tells the farmer what kinds of crops will grow best in the different soils in his land.

This is a soil capability map. It shows the different kinds of soils in an area and tells a farmer what can be done with them. This is indicated by a code made up of numbers. For example, note VII-3 in a small area at the upper left-hand part of the map. The VII means that the ground is rough, steep, and has been harmed by erosion. The 3 tells the farmer to plant soil-conserving crops every second year.

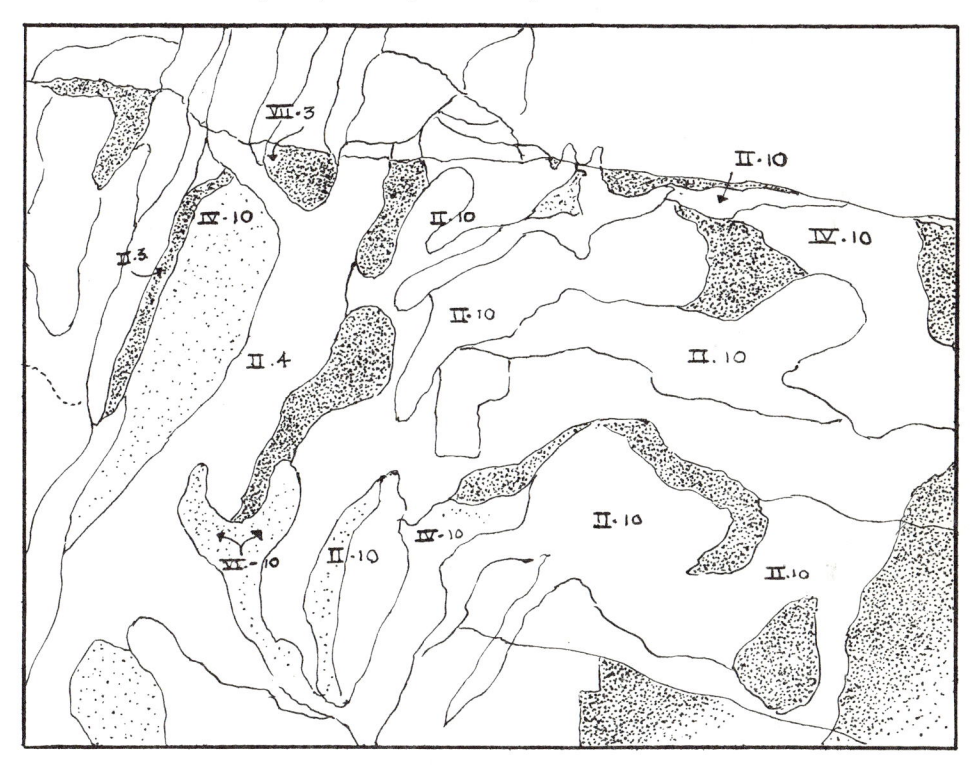

Contour Plowing and Strip Cropping

The map is also used to work out the way the field should be plowed. If there are hills, the mod-

85

The owners of these two farms use both contour plowing (left) and strip cropping (right) to prevent erosion from taking soil from their farms.

ern farmer will do *contour plowing.* This means that all the furrows will be plowed horizontally, following the shape (the contour) of the surface of the ground. The furrows will be plowed not up and down hills, but around the hills. Horizontal furrows hold rainwater and give it time to sink into the soil, instead of running downhill and forming gullies.

The farmer and the soil expert will also decide whether there should be crop rotation. Modern crop rotation usually is done by *strip cropping*. The different crops are planted in several strips. Since chemical fertilizers can be used, the main object of modern crop rotation is not so much to keep the soil from becoming worn out as to control erosion.

For example, a crop such as corn, tobacco, or cotton is planted in one strip. These crops need widely spaced furrows kept clean of weeds and are called "open" crops. An open-crop strip will suffer erosion.

But in the neighboring strip, an unplowed, close-growing crop — such as grass, clover, or soybeans — is planted. These crops cover the soil completely and protect it from raindrop erosion.

Then rainwater running off the open-crop strip is slowed down by the close-growing plants in the next strip. The slowed water drops the soil particles it is carrying and sinks into the soil.

The next year, the crops in the strips are switched, or rotated.

Finally, the soil expert will work out a program for fertilizing the soil. He will fit the fertilizers to the different kinds of soils, giving each crop what it needs by supplying what the soil lacks. He will also advise the farmer on what chemicals to use to fight any possible diseases caused by fungi or bacteria, and to control insects and nematodes that might harm the crops.

Thanks to soil science, the modern farmer no longer faces the same risks taken by the hundreds of generations of farmers before him. Scientific soil management gives the modern farmer every reason to expect good crops. And in countries that make use of soil science, the crops are the largest in history.

GLOSSARY

actinomycetes — Microscopic plants that resemble both bacteria and fungi. (*See also* bacteria *and* fungus.)
A-horizon — The top layer of soil; also called topsoil. (*See also* topsoil.)
alga (plural: algae) — Single-celled green plant that lives in water and damp places.
alkaline —-the opposite of acid.
ameba (plural: amebas) — Microscopic, single-celled animal that is constantly changing shape, and is found in soil. (*See also* protozoa.)
antibiotic — Substance produced by living things, such as actinomycetes, bacteria, and fungi, and which is used in medicine to kill or prevent the growth of harmful bacteria. (*See also* actinomycetes, bacteria, *and* fungi.)
aureomycin — Antibiotic produced from actinomycetes.
avalanche — Large mass of snow and ice, earth, or rock, sliding down a mountainside.

bacteria — Microscopic, single-celled plants without chlorophyll; the smallest of all plants.
bedrock — Solid rock beneath soil.
B-horizon — Layer of soil directly below the A-horizon; also called subsoil. (*See also* zone of accumulation.)
boulder — Rock or stone with a diameter larger than 10 inches.

carbon dioxide — Colorless, odorless, tasteless gas that makes up about three parts of every 10,000 of the atmosphere; carbon dioxide is used by green plants in the process by which they make their own food; carbon dioxide dissolves in rainwater, forming carbonic acid.
carbonic acid — Acid formed when carbon dioxide in the air dissolves in rainwater; this acid dissolves rocks in the process of weathering.
cell — A small mass of protoplasm enclosed in a membrane; the unit of which all living things are made. (*See also* protoplasm.)

cellulose — Stiff material that surrounds the cell membranes of plants.
cell wall — Cellulose covering that surrounds the cell membrane of all plant cells.
chlorophyll — Green substance that enables a green plant to make its own food (starch) from carbon dioxide and water, using energy from sunlight. (*See also* carbon dioxide.)
C-horizon — Layer of soil that is directly below the B-horizon and directly above bedrock. (*See also* bedrock.)
contour plowing — Plowing horizontal furrows that follow the shape of the land.
crop rotation — Planting an area with a harvest crop one year and a soil-renewing crop the next, and repeating this operation each year.

denitrifying bacteria — Bacteria that release nitrogen from decaying plants and animals.

erosion — Action of water or wind in changing the earth's surface.

fallow field — Field that is allowed to lie idle during a growing season in order to restore nitrogen and minerals to the soil.
flagellate — Microscopic, single-celled animal that has a threadlike bit of living matter that sticks out from the cell and is whipped back and forth, causing the animal to swim through water.
fungus (plural: fungi) — Plant that lacks chlorophyll, and therefore cannot make its own food, but gets nourishment from living or dead plants or animals.
furrow — Plowed channel between two rows of crops.

granite — Kind of rock containing quartz and other minerals. (*See also* quartz.)

larva (plural: larvae) — Stage in the life of some insects after they hatch from an egg.

legume — Plant that gets nitrogen from bacteria that live on the plant's roots in groups called nodules.
lichen — Partnership of a fungus and an alga, living as a single plant.
lime — White mineral made up of calcium carbonate. (See *also* mineral.)
limestone — Calcium carbonate in the form of rock.

mineral — Substance made up of chemical elements combined in definite proportions and found in the earth by itself or combined with other minerals, making up rocks.
mite — Very small spiderlike animal.
mold — Kind of fungus, especially one living on damp, once-living matter.
mole — Burrowing animal that lives entirely within the soil.
mycelium — Threadlike part of a mold that acts like a root.

nematode — Very small threadlike worm having a round body not divided into segments as in an earthworm.
nitrate — Nitrogen combined with other elements, making a substance that plants can use to get the nitrogen.
nitrogen — Chemical element that makes up four-fifths of the air, and is part of all living things.
nitrogen cycle — Round-and-round process in which nitrogen from the air enters soil by means of nitrogen-fixing bacteria, is taken in by plants, and is returned to the air by denitrifying bacteria, causing plant and animal matter to decay. (See *also* nitrogen-fixing bacteria *and* denitrifying bacteria.)
nitrogen-fixing bacteria — Bacteria that can make the nitrogen of the air part of their bodies.
oxygen — Chemical element that make up a little more than one-fifth of air and is needed by all animals and all but a few plants in order to live.

parasite — Plant or animal that lives on or in another, called a *host*, from which it gets food, sometimes starving or sickening the host.
pedologist — Soil scientist.

protein — Nitrogen-containing substance that is a necessary part of all plant and animal cells.

protozoa — one-celled animals. (*See also* ameba *and* flagellate.)

pupa (plural: pupae) — Resting stage in the life of an insect, in which the larva surrounds itself with a cocoon, or pupa case, and eventually emerges as a fully developed insect.

quartz — Hard, tough mineral made up of the elements silicon and oxygen.

soil capability map — Map of the different soils of an area, used to decide what crops can be grown in each kind of soil.

shrew — Small mouselike mammal with a long, pointed snout; it lives in the soil, tunneling to find worms and insects, which it eats.

spore — Single cell produced by fungi and other plants, and from which a new plant grows, as from a seed.

subsoil — Soil below the A-horizon, or topsoil.

terramycin — Antibiotic made from actinomycetes. (*See also* actinomycetes *and* antibiotic.)

topsoil — Top layer of soil, made up of a mixture of rock particles, decaying once-living materials, and living plants and animals; the A-horizon.

tundra — Treeless plain in the Arctic region, with the soil a few inches below the surface frozen even during the summer.

weathering — Process by which rocks are broken into small particles by the action of weather.

windbreak — Line of trees or bushes planted to break the force of the wind and prevent wind erosion. (*See also* erosion.)

zone of accumulation — The B-horizon, in which soil minerals accumulate upon being carried down from the surface and up from bedrock by water. (*See also* B-horizon *and* mineral.)

INDEX

A — horizon, 29-30.
  See also topsoil
acid, 84
actinomycetes, 45-46, 47
actinomycin. See antibiotics
agriculture, 67
air, 25, 27, 36, 46, 47, 49, 50, 80
alfalfa, 47
alga, 17-19
alkaline, 84
Allegheny Mountains, 58-59
amebas, 42
ammonia, 67.
  See also fertilizer, chemical
animals, 10, 15, 18, 27, 35-42, 48, 51; dead, 21, 25-26, 27, 34, 46; insectlike, 37, 39; one-celled, 35, 42
antibiotics, 46
ants, 37
aridosols. See soil, desert
ashes, 11
Assyria, 58
atmosphere, 14

B — horizon, 30, 55, 80, 84
Babylonia, Babylonians, 53-58, 62, 63, 66, 69, 72
bacteria, 20, 26, 41, 42, 46-49, 67, 89. See also denitrifying bacteria
barley, 64
beans. See legumes
bedrock, 31, 33. See also C — horizon
beetles, 37
berries, 52
bombs. See raindrops
boulders, 12
bread mold, 18, 44
burrows, 36, 40

C — horizon, 31, 33, 55
canals. See irrigation, canals
carbon, 46
carbon dioxide, 17; gas, 25
carbonic acid, 25
cattle, 26, 52, 56, 66
cell, 19, 42
centipedes, 26, 37
channels, 55
chemicals, 47, 88

chemical weathering.
  See weathering
chernozem. See soil, prairie
chiggers, 40-41
chlorophyll, 17, 18
clay, 84
climate, 27, 30, 33, 34
clouds, 14
clover, 47, 88
Colorado, 70
continent, 14, 15
contour plowing. See plowing
corn, 26, 70, 88
cotton, 77, 88
craters, 73
crops, 9-10, 33, 41, 44, 52-53, 58-59, 60-61, 62, 63-66, 68, 70-71, 77, 84; close-growing, 88; open, 88; rotation, 66, 87-88

decay, 10, 20, 21, 27, 28, 33, 36, 48, 51, 54, 63, 64, 66, 67, 79
deer, 26
denitrifying bacteria, 48-49
deserts, 23
disease, 41, 88. See also fungus
drought, 70-71
Dust Bowl, the, 70-71
dust storms, 13, 70
Dutch, 60

earth, the, 11, 20, 51; axis, 14; crust, 14, 15
earthquakes, 11
earthworms, 37
engineer, 9, 30, 54
erosion, 15, 55-56, 68, 72-80, 88
Euphrates River, 54
Europe, 70

fallow, 64-66
farmers, 9-10, 29, 52, 54-55, 58, 60, 63, 66, 68, 70-71, 86, 87, 88, 89; American, 84; European, 64
farming, 52, 58-59, 62; three-field, 64 66; two-field, 64
fertilizer, 66-67, 88; chemical, 67-68, 88
fishing, 52
flagellates, 42

flowers, 43
food, 52, 56, 62, 67
forest, 27, 34, 56, 58-59, 77
fruits, 43, 52
fungus, fungi, 17-19, 26, 44-45, 46, 48; diseases, 44, 88
furrows, 54, 55, 77, 86, 88

gases, 27, 47
goats, 56
gophers, 35
granite, 33
grass, 26, 28, 33, 34, 40, 43, 44, 52, 56-57, 60, 61, 71, 77-79, 88
gravestones, 21-22
Greece, 58, 64
ground cover, 77
gullies, 55, 59, 72, 87

Haber, Fritz, 67
herdsmen, 52, 56-57, 70
hills, 28, 34, 84-85, 86
humidity, 21
hunting, 52
hydrogen gas, 57

ice, 23
Illinois, 60
India, 58, 67-68
Indiana, 60
insects, 26, 28, 29, 35, 36-37, 39, 89; eggs, 36
Iraq, 53
irrigation, 54; canals, 54, 57-58

Kansas, 70

land, 18, 34
larva, larvae, 36
lava, 11
leaves, 26, 28, 40, 43, 44, 79
legumes, 47-48, 64-66, 67
lichens, 16-20. See also alga, fungus
lightning, 13
lime, 33
limestone, 33
living, 9-10

mammals, 35, 41
manure, 66. See also fertilizer
materials, once-living, 19-20, 46. See also plants, animals
meat, 70
mechanical weathering. See weathering
medicine, 46

mice, 26, 35-36
microscope, 35, 46
Middle Ages, the, 64
millipedes, 37
minerals, 30, 33, 34, 43, 54-55, 63, 66, 67
mites, 26, 37, 40-41
moisture, 18, 19, 50
mold, 26
moles, 35-36
mollisols. See soil, prairie
mountains, 11, 23, 56
mud, 57, 58, 75, 79, 82
mulch, 66
mushrooms, 18
mycelium, 44

nematodes, 41, 89. See also worms, threadworms
New Jersey, 60
New Mexico, 70
New York, 70
nitrates, 48, 67
nitrogen, 46, 47-48, 54-55, 63, 66, 67, 68; gas, 49
nitrogen cycle, 49
nitrogen-fixing bacteria, 47-48, 64
nodules, 47
nonliving, 9-10
nuts, 52

ocean, 14, 15, 18
Ohio, 60
Oklahoma, 70
oxidation, 27
oxygen, 27, 67

parasites, 40-41
parks, 37
particles, 9, 41, 47, 70, 71, 74, 80, 88; rock, 10, 80
partnership. See lichens
pasture, 56, 70
peanuts, 47
peas. See legumes
pedology. See soil, science
Persia, 58
phosphorus, 67
plants, 10, 15, 18, 20, 27, 35, 41, 43-51, 68, 77-79; dead, 21, 25-26, 27, 34, 41; reproduction of, 50-51
plowing, 85; contour, 85
podzols. See soils, forest

95

poison, 68
potassium, 67
prairie dogs, 35
prairies, 60
proteins, 48
protozoa, 42. *See also* amebas, flagellates
pupa, pupae, 36, 37

quartz, 30

rain, 13, 14, 21, 25, 29, 54, 57; erosion, 71, 72-80
raindrops, 14, 25, 72-80
rainwater, 14, 22-23, 30, 34, 48, 55, 56, 59, 61-62, 87-88
rivers, 14, 15
rock, 9, 12, 15-16, 18, 19, 20, 21, 23, 30, 31, 34, 43; decomposition of, 25; dust, 15, 19, 20, 28; grains, 20, 28; molten, 11; solid, 11
Rome, 58, 64
roots, 28, 30, 35, 36, 41, 43-44, 47, 52, 54, 64, 67, 77
rotting, 28
roundworms, 41

sand, 10, 12, 33, 84
sand storms, 13
scientist, soil, 10, 11, 15, 16, 18, 29, 31, 34, 40, 71, 72, 75, 77, 84, 87-89
seasons, 15, 31, 53-54, 55
seaweed, 18-19
seeds, 19, 26, 28, 29, 35, 36, 50-51; coats, 26, 43, 50; germinating of, 43
sheep, 56, 66
sheet erosion, 72
shrews, 35-36
silt, 80
sod. *See* grass
soil, 9-11, 15-16, 23, 27, 36, 42, 46, 51, 53, 54; conservation, 63; desert, 33; experts, 60; forest, 33, 34; horizons, 29-33; kinds of, 31-34, 84; prairie, 31-33, 34; reclaiming of, 62; science, 63, 89; theories about, 16-20
soil capability map, 84, 85
soil-making process, 20, 21-27
sow bugs, 37
soy beans, 47, 88

spiders, 37, 40
spodosols. *See* soils, forest
spores, 19
springtails, 37
steam, 14
stems, 43, 44, 79
strands, 9, 17
streams, 14, 15, 72; underground, 30-31
strip cropping, 87-88
subsoil, 55, 80-83
sun, 13, 14, 17, 23, 44, 70

temperature, 11, 14-15, 19, 21, 23, 31, 34, 50
terramycin. *See* antibiotics
Texas, 70
threadworms, 41
thunderstorms, 13
ticks, 40-41
Tigris River, 54
tobacco, 88
topsoil, 29, 31-33, 56, 62, 70, 80-83. *See also* A — Horizon
trees, 43, 56, 61, 71, 77; evergreen, 33
tunnels, 36, 40
turf. *See* grass
twigs, 26, 28

United States, 33, 34, 58-61, 68, 69-71
United States Soil Conservation Service, 84

volcanoes, 11, 13
vegetables, 64

Washington, 70
water, 9, 18, 25, 27, 30, 42, 43, 44, 46, 47, 67
water erosion. *See* erosion
weather, 15, 21, 68
weathering, 21-25, 30, 31, 34, 51
weeds, 55, 63, 64, 88
wheat, 26, 64, 70
wind, 12, 14, 21, 56, 61, 71; erosion, 56, 68-71
windbreaks, 71
wireworms, 37
World War I, 70
worms, 26, 29, 36, 40. *See also* earthworms, threadworms, roundworms, wireworms

zone of accumulation. *See* B — Horizon

96